With appreciation,
your friendship and a...

DAVE Bowman

Gordon Gekko: CEO

Lessons from Wall Street for a Winning Attitude

David L. Bowman & Douglas E. Hess

Dedications

From Dave:

I dedicate this book to my wife, Lynda, and our three
boys Joshua, Jacob and Joseph. Each of you is more
precious to me than words can express. I love you all
and I cannot imagine a happier life than the one I have
with each of you!

To my Mom: thank you for always believing in me and
encouraging me.

Thanks to my Dad and Stepmom; you've set a spiritual
example that I will always cherish.

To my entire family: I will always love you!!

From Doug:

I dedicate this book to my wife, Misty and our two boys
Zack and Drew. You are the inspiration that drives me
to be the best I can be.

To my parents: you have given me a strong work ethic
and encouraged me to dream. Thank you for always
believing in me. I love you! Dad, I miss you everyday
and I look forward to when we are reunited.

From Both:

To God: we thank you for showing us what love really looks like. And for the countless blessings we experience on a daily basis!

Contents

Introduction

This is the second edition of this book. It's been revised
and expanded to include an additional chapter and a few
updates to some of the original chapters. Nor did the
first edition include this introduction. We thank those of
you who asked how the book came to fruition and how
we came to know each other; your comments have
inspired this introduction. We also want to thank you for
reporting to us how this book inspired you. We hope
you find additional benefit in this second edition and we
hope new readers will be as inspired too!

It's odd that a movie about corporate greed and the
immoral, illegal act of insider trading can serve as a
motivator for a book about business ethics, hard work,
and building a proper attitude for success. But if that
isn't the epitome of "out-of-the-box thinking" we feel
you would be hard pressed to find another example
among non-fiction literature. It is a bit of a challenge to
view the world in such a way that you can see through
the negative and focus on what is positive. But that is
exactly the aim of this book.

First, let us share with you how the authors came to
know each other and how this book came to fruition.
The authors both arrived at the same company through
different paths and ended up working together side-by-
side. Dave as the Regional Director over an assigned

territory and Doug as one of the Senior Marketing Associates reporting to him. The two became, and still remain, good friends.

While attending a motivational seminar together Doug commented that he had an idea for a book. Doug loves the movie Wall Street and constantly quotes the film. He said to Dave, "You know how I'm always quoting the movie Wall Street? I've thought about putting those quotes into a book that shares what those quotes mean to me." Dave encouraged Doug to move forward with that idea. He believed it was marketable because of the popularity of the movie and felt it could serve to motivate others.

Now, if you've ever written something, you know that it is not always easy. Even prolific, professional writers have writer's block and can find it difficult to put their ideas onto paper sometimes. The process was no different for this endeavor. Doug was sharing this frustration with Dave and invited him to be a part of the project. Dave agreed. You are now reading the outcome of this collaboration.

We did not set out with grandiose plans to write a book that would change the world. In fact, the subtitle of the book was created during the writing process because we realized that although what we were writing was from a different perspective than what the movie portrayed, it was not new. They had written a movie and used the very quotes that served as our subject for each chapter; of course, it wasn't new. However, we wanted to share the positive aspects of what those quotes meant to us as we worked together as authors, and as employees of the same company serving the same territory. We wanted people to realize you can always see the positive, even in the most negative of circumstances, and apply that positivity to your life. We wanted the book to serve as inspiration to encourage people to look for the best in themselves and others, to work hard, to never give up, and to develop a winning attitude! In this endeavor, we have succeeded!

Chapter 1

Every Dream has a Price

"Life all comes down to a few moments. This is one of them."
– Bud Fox

Do you have a dream? Do you want to develop the winning attitude that will help you succeed? You're not alone. Jake Neuberg and Ramit Varma both shared a dream too. Here's their story (As taken from their website):

Jake and Ramit met at UCLA's Anderson School of Business where they realized that while they both had business backgrounds, they'd also both spent significant time as SAT prep tutors, Jake at Kaplan and Ramit at Princeton Review. They also realized they both felt that something was missing from the big tutoring companies. So, Jake and Ramit came up with an idea ... a revolutionary idea. Together, they decided to start a new test prep company, one that was completely different from the two market leaders.

They started their company with no outside investment. At first, they ran Revolution Prep out of Jake's apartment and paid for everything with newly-opened credit cards. This meant late nights, high risk, and mounting debt. This meant answering every phone call themselves. It even meant having their phones turned off temporarily because they'd missed a payment. But it also meant individual attention for every customer and complete involvement from Jake and Ramit. It meant they threw themselves into the company and acted like every potential new client was a make-or-break situation, because in a way it was.

They were the scrappy underdog in the test prep world. At times, they couldn't help wondering if they were crazy for giving up the security and big pay checks of consulting or investment jobs. But the passion they felt for their new business and the fact that they knew they could do a better job helping students achieve success than the existing companies, kept them going.

In just a few years, Revolution Prep became the leading SAT and ACT test prep company in California. And how did they manage to accomplish this? By trying new things, being flexible, listening carefully to customers, and committing to the social mission of never denying a student the chance to take a Revolution Prep class, even if that student could not pay for the class.

Revolution turned the old test prep model on its head. Instead of focusing only on teaching students tricks to "beat" the test, Revolution teaches long-term learning strategies and ways to alleviate test-day stress. Instead of spending money on specialized testing centers, Revolution partners with high schools to hold classes at the schools, making the classes much more convenient for students. And Revolution has stuck to its promise: never turn away a student who wants to take a test prep course but cannot pay. They do this, Jake explains, "because it's the right thing to do."

Jake and Ramit set a lofty goal for their company. They didn't want to create just a test prep company that helped students prepare for college admissions tests; they wanted to create a transformative educational company which empowers students to take control of their education and teaches them to become better learners.

As Revolution Prep has continued to develop new and innovative products, it has increased in size, revenue, and scope. But one thing that hasn't changed is its mission: to revolutionize the test prep industry and help as many students as possible. Revolution, now a major competitor in the education services industry, still has the attitude and work ethic of the scrappy underdog it used to be.

We dream and imagine all the time. Our heads are constantly filled with ideas. The world is full of great ideas and dreams, but most are never even close to being fulfilled because most people are afraid of failing or having to give up something in return. We have a good friend, an author of three entrepreneurial books, who once said to us, "Good ideas are a dime a dozen but folks willing to follow through on those ideas and make the necessary sacrifices are rare." Too often people are not willing to pay the price to make their dreams come true.

Before you decide to pursue your dream - whatever it may be - you have to consider the "price" you will have to pay to bring your dream to fruition. When we say price we're sure you realize we don't mean only a literal financial cost; although that may be necessary. We're sure you realize we're talking about the price as Webster defines it: "that which must be given, or undergone, in order to obtain a thing." In a word, Sacrifice.

Those sacrifices aren't going to be easy or they wouldn't call them "Sacrifices". A sacrifice is never easy and more often than not it affects another person. If you're willing to give up your time, are you the only person from whom you are taking time away? Perhaps, the sacrifice of your time will also mean a sacrifice for your family. How many sporting events, recitals, scout meetings, and other activities will you be missing to pursue your dream? Is your dream worth it to you to make those sacrifices?

Consider a young single mother who wants to make a better life for herself and her kids by increasing her education. While the decision to go back to school is an admirable one, and worthy of pursuing, what price will this mother have to pay to make it happen? Certainly there will be the financial burden of paying for the education. Most likely there will also be times when she will have to be away from her children when she really wants to be there with them. Perhaps she will even make the sacrifice of a lesser grade rather than to miss something she knows is important to her kids; something they want to share with her, and it will be heartbreaking for them if she misses it. As you can see your sacrifice can be made on opposite sides of the same coin. In this case, return to school missing time spent and memories built with kids in exchange for an education, or choose lower grades in exchange for less study and more time with children.

What decision will the mother make? Only she can answer that question. Just as only you can answer the questions regarding the decision you will make when it comes to your dream. Have you considered your sacrifices? It's going to take some introspection. Too many times we are looking for people to give us an answer. "Tell me what to do, please!" Consultation is good but, ultimately, you have to make the decision regarding your own dream and the sacrifices you are willing to make.

We're not trying to dissuade you from moving forward and making your dream a reality; we're just asking you to consider how your decision will impact others. Yes, the sacrifices can be great but the rewards can make them worthwhile!

Many people are able to compartmentalize their time and pursue their dream while still being there for their families and even participating in hobbies, unrelated to their dream, that bring them joy. We hope you are one of those folks. But keep in mind that even those lucky few often make a painful sacrifice at some point in the journey. For some people, it's a breaking point that causes everything they hoped for to come crashing in around them.

It is rare that something of value comes easily to us. We all hear stories of people who were in the right place at the right time. "Man, that guy is really lucky!" we might say to ourselves. But is it really luck?

We once heard a story about a young man who wanted to buy a car. He was willing to spend about $1,000. This was in the early 1980's so a thousand dollars would have bought a decent used car for a first-time car owner.

He searched the papers and viewed dozens of cars

looking for the car he knew was right for him. He didn't

expect anything too fancy just a good solid car in good

running condition. Most of the cars were nice but he

knew looking at them he would not be happy driving

them for long and he wanted something that he was

going to be happy owning and would enjoy driving. He

turned down many cars that most other young men his

age would have snapped up quickly. One day while

looking through the paper he found this advertisement:

"1959 Chevy. Needs tires. $350." He wasn't exactly

looking for a 1959 Chevy, and especially one needing

tires, but the price was right and with $1,000 as his

budget he thought if everything else seemed good he

could cover the price of the tires and still come in way
under budget, so he decided to check it out.

He arrived at the house and an elderly woman answered
the door. The young man mentioned he was calling
about the car and she said it was her husbands. She
explained how her husband had been working on it in the
barn but he died a few months earlier. She escorted the
young man to the barn and opened the big barn door for
him. His eyes widened as the light fell on a 1959 Chevy
Corvette in near pristine condition except that it was
sitting on blocks needing tires. He immediately said "I'll
take it!"

For less than $1,000 dollars this young man found a
dream car that turned heads wherever he drove it. It
would be easy to think he was just in the right place at
the right time or got really lucky. And that would be

partly true because the woman who sold the car only knew that it was a Chevy and was not concerned with the model. She felt $350 was a fair price for a 20+ year old car regardless of make and model. But let's look at some of the sacrifices this young man made as he searched for his first car. We can start with the fact that he wouldn't settle for something he felt wasn't right for him just to get a car. How many times are we in such a rush to get what we want that we are willing to settle for the first thing that comes along? Secondly, he sacrificed his time to look at dozens of cars and yet never tired of saying "no" to something he didn't want or wasn't right for his needs. How many times do we just get tired of waiting and eventually choose something "good enough" but not exactly what we were looking for? And lastly, he didn't give up but remained confident that he would find "the right car." How many times do we give up because things seem to take too long, are too hard, or we feel it will just never happen?

If you choose to go through life settling for less than your best, unwilling to make the sacrifices necessary to bring your dream to reality, then you will stand among the many who never achieve their dream. You can count yourself among the "dime-a-dozen crowd" who never follow through on their good idea.

However, if you are willing to make the sacrifices of time, money, personal interests, or whatever you've determined will have to be your individual sacrifices then you can succeed. Most importantly, never settle for something that isn't "right". Never accept "good enough" when you are tired. And never quit when things get harder than you expected them. If you stick to these principles and make the necessary sacrifices, then you can achieve your dream and make it a reality! Every dream has a price. Are you willing to pay it?

Chapter One's Advice for Life

Be prepared to make a sacrifice.

Know what you are willing to sacrifice.

Be a person of action.

Start immediately.

Make the most of every moment.

Be flexible when you see benefit in compromise.

Try new things; think outside the box.

Have a mission – beyond just making money.

Don't be afraid to fail but learn from it.

Do not settle for less than you want/need.

Be confident; stand tall, literally (it builds confidence).

Use your imagination.

Think big.

Ignore discouragement, even from yourself.

Resolve to succeed.

Chapter 2

<u>Money Never Sleeps</u>

"The main thing about money, Bud, is that it makes you do things you don't want to do" - Lou Mannheim

Too many times individuals obtain a small amount of success and then they sit back and rest on their laurels. Success is a wonderful thing, but one must keep that success alive. Let success breed success by capitalizing on existing momentum.

In the quote above by Lou Mannheim there is much to be gleaned. If you look at it closely, you realize there are multiple ways of interpreting what is being said.

When its first read many people will see the comment as a negative, perhaps inferring that money makes you do bad things. Well, they would be right because money has made many people do bad things. Many people believe there is an evil power behind money that seeks to control us. However, there are also many folks who have more money than they can ever spend and yet they have earned it honestly and use it as a tool to do good works.

The other way to interpret the quote is that money can motivate you to do the things you would otherwise feel are too hard to do or not worth doing without the benefit of the reward; in this case, money. However, money doesn't have to be your motivator and it's probably better if it isn't your sole motivator.

The difference between these two interpretations probably has to do with your opinion of money. For some, money is just a tool they use to do good things for themselves and others. Much like any tool, you would be disappointed if you lost it but it's not what you live for. Others see money in an entirely different way; they don't see it as a tool as much as a symbol. They may use it to buy other status symbols such as expensive cars, boats, homes or clothing. Some may just want to see a giant number on their statement each month and never spend the money on themselves nor others. Your opinion of money may determine how you use it and how you allow it to motivate you.

That said, the authors of this book are choosing to use the term "money never sleeps" but for the sake of this chapter, you can replace money with those things that motivate you and help you to define success in your own terms. Whatever you will have accomplished to allow you to say you've succeeded and achieved your goals is what you need to put in place of our reference to money. This chapter is not about money; it is about hard work.

Before we jump into some of the nitty-gritty regarding how to make working hard work FOR you rather than just taking up your time, let's start with a true story that happened to one of the authors, Doug Hess:

It is not uncommon in our industry to travel for customer appointments and time on the road means many nights in a hotel room and away from your family. One night while traveling Doug left his blackberry device turned on and charging on the nightstand next to the bed. Around 2:00 AM he was awakened by the gentle buzzing of an incoming email.

He reached over to see who was sending an email at this time of night. Anticipating the email to be a SPAM, he was surprised to learn that a client had sent a few questions about some items they had discussed a few days earlier. (It should be noted that the client later told Doug that he was up with his 6-month-old baby and decided "why not work a little?"). Doug quickly wrote an email back to the client stating he would reply after looking into the questions first thing in the morning when the systems were up and internal staff members would be available to discuss the questions.

Well, long story short, the questions were answered very early the next morning and the client couldn't have been happier that their questions were answered timely and they knew within a few minutes of sending them, they were received and would be looked into as soon as possible.

Doug went on to take some ribbing from both the client and internal staff about sleeping with his blackberry but the story secured two things for Doug; it secured the client and it secured a reputation within the industry that he worked harder and longer than those who performed the same functions for other companies. As a result, additional clients were secured simply based on their perception that the level of service they would receive from Doug and, consequently, our company would be superior if only for the ability to reach someone.

The story above is a perfect example of the motto "Money Never Sleeps". Constantly believe you are behind in the game and are trying to play catch up. Every day you should assume that your competition is two hours ahead of you on the road, or in the office two hours before you, or staying two hours after your computer is logged off each night. If you work like you're behind, then you'll soon lap your competition!

Please do not misunderstand what we're saying here. It is imperative to "power down" from the office. If you don't, there is a real chance you are going to lose your family, burn out too quickly, or in the worst case scenario, send yourself to an early grave. Please know it is okay to "power down" but just don't "power off" completely. Take the necessary breaks to keep your sanity and be there for your family. If you can't do good things with your family and/or friends, then for what are you working? It does you no good if you can't share your success and the fruit it bears?

We're going to belabor this point just a bit because money, or the effort to earn it, will require you to do things you do not necessarily want to do, professionally speaking. Although most of us are willing to put in a good day's work to earn our pay it's not too often you'll find someone who is willing to put in extra effort to bring about their own success. We'll remind you here of chapter one and making the necessary sacrifices to succeed. Every entrepreneur knows that building a business takes much more effort than it appears from the outside.

The nice thing is you don't have to do it alone. In fact, you may want to seriously consider getting a few folks to share in seeing you achieve your success. Most people want to help and see someone succeed. If you doubt that statement, then just watch the *"Price is Right"* or other game shows that focus on only one contestant at a time. In nearly every case, we want to see the contestant succeed. People will help you if given the chance.

While on a three day travel swing visiting clients we stopped in to see one of our long term clients. We spoke for a while and just before we got ready to leave we asked the question that we normally ask each client, "Do you need anything." This client thought for a few minutes then stated that they could use a few pens, highlighters, etc... Well, we usually carry these items with us in the trunk of the car, but on this trip for some reason we didn't have any supplies with us. So, we mentioned that we would be on the road traveling but when we got back into the office we would make sure we sent the items requested. Once, we left the client's office we got into the car and started to work. We made a call to our internal staff and asked them to send the requested items along with a handwritten note to the client from us. Since, we were not in the office to write the note, we asked the staff member to stop any guy within the office and hand write the message and then we dictated to her what we wanted the note to say and to make sure that our signature was attached. We also knew that the package would be delivered by end of business the next day, providing there wasn't a delay caused by the shipping company.

Sure enough, we received a call from the client the very next day stating she had received the items and asking how we were able to get them delivered to her so quickly. We didn't go into details but simply stated that "We're here to exceed your expectations" and to let us know what more we could do for her.

The client was happy and we shared the story with our internal folks and shared our sincere appreciation for their help. They were pleased to know their efforts had helped and that we had satisfied a client that would continue to remain loyal to our company because we worked together and continued to exceed expectations!

Most people are not willing to work that hard; they won't do it for themselves nor their customers, but those who are willing can yield results most other folks will only dream about. Why, because your customers expect it from you. It's not uncommon today for people to make promises they never deliver. But we're suggesting you actually under-promise and over-deliver for those you serve. It will get their attention and get you noticed. It will also earn their business and support.

For you sports fans we'll say it this way: would you be thrilled with your favorite team if they just showed up to play moments before the game started? No, you would be outraged! You, as a fan, expect your team, or favorite athlete, to have arrived early to warm up and get focused for the game. You expect your team to have worked harder, practiced more, and be aware of the strengths and weaknesses of their opponents. How is that any different from your clients? They too expect you to arrive early and be focused on the task ahead. They want you to be able to display for them why they should "root" for you rather than your competition. Are you ready to show them?

Just keep in mind that someone is always working somewhere. If you want to get noticed for being the winner that you are, then you need to work hard to always be the fastest to reply and make yourself as available as possible to those you serve (or wish to someday). You need to position your efforts so that they are always working for you even when you are "powered down". Perhaps that means placing a phone call after everyone has left for the day so your message is the first one your client will hear in the morning. Or consider sending something in the mail so that the post office is working for you while you're away from the office. The point is, do things that exceed the expectations of others and do them quickly! Money never sleeps; and neither should your efforts!

Chapter Two's Advice for Life

Work hard.

Challenge yourself.

Be prepared.

Do not allow money to be your only motivation.

Use money as a tool for outcomes.

Put in extra effort.

Capitalize on existing momentum.

Take a break once in a while.

Find good mentors.

Be helpful; seek to bring improvement to others' situations.

Exceed expectations.

Chapter 3

The Most Valuable Commodity is Information

"The most valuable commodity I know of is

information." – Gordon Gekko

Do you remember the year you bought your first Personal Computer? What was the primary use of that computer? If you're like most people it was to play Solitaire or Minesweeper. Oh sure, some people used it for keeping track of their personal financial records on spreadsheets and backed them up on "floppy disks" but most used their computer as simply another expensive toy. Things may not have changed too much regarding how we use our computers but what we can use them for has expanded tremendously.

The internet has expanded our access to information in such a profound way that to believe the amount of information we now have access to could have been collected so quickly and from so many different sources would have been thought impossible just a few decades ago. But now we can collect and share data within seconds and have near-instant access to information that previously would have been impossible to collect or, at the very least, incredibly slow to collect. The shear amount of time it took to collect data sometimes made the information obsolete by the time we obtained possession of it.

We have access to more information than we could have ever dreamed in the last century, and yet, so many individuals misunderstand the value of this commodity!

So many times we place preference on the wrong commodity: oil, gold, silver or something else. However, we believe INFORMATION tops them all. What makes us say this? Information puts you in the driver's seat toward success. Without good information how will you know in what direction you need to move?

Yes, we all have access to information. But do we truly understand the value of information and how to get it? Gossip, placing a phone call, sending emails, eavesdropping they are all forms of gaining knowledge, but as Gordon Gekko states to young Bud Fox, "You stop sending me information, and start getting me some". In context, he means stop sending me what I already know and tell me something I don't know. Ask yourself this question about your own collection of information: "Am I getting valuable information that is shared with only a select few or am I gathering common knowledge made available to everyone?"

If you're not getting the "insider" information for your industry then there is a high probability that you are finding yourself constantly losing business to someone. You may find yourself saying things like, "That guy is

so lucky, he's always in the right place at the right time."
Or perhaps something like, "I hate that guy. He's such a
liar!" Although it's very true that some people are
indeed in the right place at the right time and others will
use dishonest measures to get ahead. It's also possible
that your nemesis is simply getting the information he or
she needs to place themselves where they need to be in
the mind of their customer. Right now you should be
asking yourself, "How do I gather the information I need
to gain success with my customers and what do I do with
it once I have it?" Good question. Here's what we
believe will help you win when it comes to being the
trusted source of information for your customer and the
person to whom they will want to open up and share
what information they have gathered too. Including
information they have gathered about your competition!

The authors of this book attend many conferences and tradeshows. We have learned that most business deals are done in "the halls". What do we mean by "the halls"? Well, very specifically we do mean literally the halls outside of the rooms where the break-out sessions are being held but we're not limiting it to those types of halls. While many individuals will go to meetings or sessions seeking the latest news, techniques, or updates, we like to keep in touch with clients by talking over a cup of coffee, a meal or on a leisurely stroll to see the sites of the city away from the conference; this is where the true information comes out, away from their colleagues and the eavesdropping ears and probing eyes of others.

Do your best to get your client or potential customer away from the other folks with whom they work, especially your competition, and get them to a secluded area where they will feel free to talk. Now this assumes you already have a trusted and friendly relationship with the individual to whom you will be talking. If you haven't developed that relationship yet, then you need to work on building your relationship with your client as a trusted person from whom they can obtain the truth. To do this you will have to be willing to share information with them regarding knowledge they may not yet have been made aware.

At first this can be some of that common knowledge available to everyone via newsletters or trade publications. You can use that to your advantage by trying to pull out only the information you know is going to be extremely useful and interesting to your client. Once you have it compiled send it to them neatly packaged and easy to read. This will make their job easier and start you on the road to becoming their trusted resource for knowledge. It will also be a superb idea for you to also send other articles that you know will be of personal interest to your client. Send them pieces of information or articles that pertain to a specific hobby or sport you know they enjoy. This not only helps build the professional rapport between you and your client but it also builds the relationship on a personal level. And believe it or not, your customer will see your personal interest in their hobby as an indication of how well you listen to them and perceive their situation.

As you move forward with these efforts please keep in mind most individuals love to share information. It makes them feel as though they are in the know. Even if you have already heard the information they are sharing, act as if you are hearing it for the first time. If you're wondering why you shouldn't just say you have already heard what their sharing it's because, if you do, the individual sharing his or her knowledge with you will be less likely to share additional information in the future. This is important because everyone loves to be the first to share something they deem important. People love to inform others. Always tell them how much you appreciate the information they have shared. It is also important to maintain the precious balance of being in the loop yet not appearing as though you are always in tune. No one wishes to be targeted as being "outside the loop" because people may not be willing to share. The tactics we mentioned in building the relationship in the last paragraph will help you become a person viewed as "in the loop."

One thing to always remember - be honest! After Gordon Gekko lectures Bud Fox on the value of getting him information, we find Bud going to extreme effort to collect the information. You will remember some of his tactics were simply illegal. We do not suggest that you use any illegal, unethical, or immoral activities to collect information. There are many ways to get the same information without crossing any illegal or unethical boundaries. Nor do we suggest that you use information that is in itself illegal or unethical for you to have. Sharing information that is misleading or dishonest for you to have in your possession will do more damage to you than any perceived advantage of sharing it in the first place. You will never be trusted again and your actions will spread like wildfire through your industry and your company.

As far as obtaining the information in a legal and ethical way based on personal relationships, trust, and shared interest then the person you may always want to consider starting with is the Administrative Assistant. You may have heard the saying "it is really the administrative assistant that truly runs the office." Well, we believe it is true and have experienced that they talk to everyone they perceive as "in the loop". They control the flow and, in some cases, even the mood of the office. Your more seasoned assistant is probably very aware of this and likely wears it as a badge of honor. These long-time gatekeepers are a little difficult to extract information from, but it is not impossible. To get information from these folks will require time, persistence, trust and patience. But once you have them in your corner you can count yourself as an "insider". However, most of them, if not all of them, will put you through a series of tests to see if you can be trusted. Be sincere and be yourself and above all as Gekko says, "save the cheap salesman talk". They will not only see right through you but they will enjoy tearing you apart and keeping you from ever entering into the inner sanctum.

Finally, when someone tells you something in confidence, keep it that way. Once you reveal a source, no one will ever be a source for you again.

So, here's your task, gather as much information from the "common knowledge" sources you have available to you right now. Share that information in a concise and easy to read way with your clients or potential customers. After sending them some industry information, send them at least one item, an article perhaps, that pertains to a personal interest they have of which they have made you aware. If it didn't come up in your conversation tell via a personal note when you send the information to them that you "noticed they seem to like (insert interest here) while you were in their office." This will help make you appear to them as observant. Follow up to ensure they have received the information and ask for their feedback regarding their thoughts on current trends, based on the information you sent.

Repeat this process as you move forward in establishing yourself as the trusted resource for information and they will be willing to share with you everything they know just to keep up with you! Information is the most valuable commodity! Do you have enough of it?

Chapter Three's Advice for Life

Seek Information.

Gain knowledge, not just results.

Read – everything (Especially your industry's news).

Seek first to understand.

Ask questions.

Use good information to guide your decision-making.

Share knowledge and information but keep confidential info confidential.

Build trust.

Become a trusted source for industry information.

Talk to "underlings".

Be appreciative when info is shared with you.

Always be honest.

Chapter 4

<u>Poor, Smart and Hungry</u>

"What's worth doing is worth doing for money!" –

Gordon Gekko

Poor:

In my part of town it seemed every kid was on the government lunch plan. We all stood in line with our lunch tickets waiting to get our free meal. Oh, we had the occasional "sack-lunch kid" who brought his own lunch in his little brown bag with his name written on it so no one would pick it up by mistake. No one ever did. Most of the rest of us received a hot meal paid for on the tax-payer dime. We didn't think anything about it. In fact, we felt sorry for the kid who had to bring his own lunch.

A few new "school clothes" were purchased at the beginning of the school year but many of my clothes were bought at second-hand stores and thrift stores. Most of the new stuff we wanted for birthdays and Christmas were placed into "lay-away" allowing my mom to make payments over weeks or months. We were poor.

The problem with being poor in my neighborhood was that you didn't often know it. It seemed everybody struggled with the same things from a financial perspective. You bought what worked at the most reasonable price; no name brands here. Name brands were for people who lived in a different part of the city. I still remember the first kid who showed up at school in a new pair of Nike's. They were nylon instead of leather and an unusual color, but he was the "talk of the town" around the halls for a few days!

Often, movies and books try to capture what I call the "innocence of poverty" by portraying families in a, we-enjoy-each-other-more-than-things light and glorifying the simpler times of days past. That works really well in the movies but in real life the struggle for financial peace brings more heartache than happiness. When people look at the reasons for divorce, financial hardship and disagreements over money are always near the top of the list. One only has to watch a family torn apart because of bad decisions revolving around money to see that having it is usually better than being broke all the time. Struggling to make ends meet is seldom glamorous and many, unfortunately, never experience the "Hollywood Happy Ending" of escaping from the poverty into which they were born.

Now perhaps as you read this you may be saying to yourself, "My family didn't have to struggle. Our bills were always paid on time, no one ever broke into our house and stole Christmas presents and all of my clothes were brand new, including my leather Nike's." Well, please know there is still much you can get from this chapter even if you didn't have a poor upbringing. Let me first ask you these questions: Did you always get everything you ever wanted? Did you have to work to get some of the things you have today? Do you still want some things that you never received or earned?

If you answered yes to the first question, then you were either born with a very large silver spoon in your mouth, you're not being completely honest with yourself, or you have very modest wants. If you answered yes to the second question, then you understand the value of a dollar and have some idea of the effort it takes to obtain tangible items without resorting to crime. If you answered yes to the last question, then reading this book will help you gain the attitude it takes to keep working to obtain those things!

Here's a story specific to one of the authors, Dave Bowman: When I was fifteen I decided I wanted a Porsche. I didn't have a particular model picked out but I liked the 911 because it was the most popular but truthfully, at that time, any Porsche would do because driving a car with that name on it meant you were successful! I couldn't have put it into these words at the time but success, and a way to show people I had earned it, is what I was seeking. And isn't that what most of us are seeking? For some people it's monetary success and all the toys that go with it, while for others it may mean academic success and the approval of your peers. The vast majority of us want to be successful and have a way to demonstrate our success to others. It's what drives us. What drives you? What does success look like to you?

Today, I have my Porsche. It's a Boxster S and I love it! But if I had allowed the Porsche to be my only measure of financial success then I guess I would be done now. Fortunately, I want other things too and I'm still working to get them. And financial success is not the only goal I have. This book is another success for which I'm working. I want to be able to put on my list of accomplishments that I'm a published author.

In the end there are many ways a person can use the word "poor" to define their status. For example, you can be fiscally poor, you can be poor in spirit or you can be poor in regards to the scruples that guide your actions. In what area would you say you are poor? Whatever that area might be, ask yourself: What do I need to do to gain more in that area?

Once you have the answer to that question then you'll need to make the effort to go out and work to obtain it. There is nothing holding you back but you. And only you can decide to move forward. There is an area in which you want to gain riches. Maybe you want your dream car, a bigger house or your current one paid off; perhaps you want a boat or some other "toy" that many people will never have. It's possible you want to gain more knowledge or earn a specific degree or some other credential. Do not end up like the folks who never have the things they want because they give up on themselves.

You're poor in some way because you don't have EVERYTHING you ever wanted. What's stopping you from getting it? You are stopping you! Remember that old saying "Quitters never win and winners never quit!"? Yes, it's cliché but do you know why phrases become cliché? Because they are true! You don't have to stay poor. You just have to resolve that you will not stop until you obtain the "riches" you are seeking. Stop wasting your own time doing nothing to improve your situation. Poor is not glamorous. Get out there and find a way to make your dream come true!

<u>Smart</u>:

So how smart does a person have to be to achieve success? It's true that most CEO's of Fortune 500 companies have at least one graduate-level degree. But on the other side of that coin, there are many "uneducated" successful business owners who make just as much money running their own business! There are some MBA's that never make it out of the mailroom of their existing company and other mailroom workers who create successful courier services. Why? We believe it has to do with the perception one has of themselves and their own abilities, and also the way others perceive that person's abilities.

Imagine a twenty-two year old recent college graduate, who earned a 4.0 GPA while in school, lands a job in a good company with lots of potential for growth. If that person spends most of their time at work only completing their tasks and then flirting with the other singles in the office and planning for the weekend, it's not likely to reflect well to their boss. Sure they may get the job done and even perform it well but if that person doesn't display some desire for advancement and a willingness to take extra steps to improve themselves, and also their department and the company as a whole, they may never find recognition in a promotion or even an above average increase in their salary.

Employers want people who are going to work to make the company better! Yes, they care about your success, because your success means more for their company! Seldom do they care about what you know or how much you know. It is important during the job interview and the first stages of your new position to show that you've accomplished tasks successfully in prior positions or in school. However, most employers are not looking for the know-it-all college star who thinks he can run the company better than the CEO. Most employers need to know, or at least believe, you can do the job you're being hired to perform. After that, they want to be able to train you to perform the task their preferred way. It doesn't mean you can't be creative or find a better way that yields more success, you can. In fact, be open to sharing your ideas and prepared to explain why you think your way is better but never do it at the expense of another worker and always be motivated to improve the process for everyone. Trust us, you'll receive the recognition you deserve!

What we're saying is do not think you are above everyone else or indispensable. You're not. Companies hire very smart people all the time. Some of them are recognized as highly competent while others are largely seen as just good performers. What makes the difference? We believe it's having enough intelligence to recognize what needs to be done, when to do it, and looking for ways to improve it. If you do that for your boss, you'll always be seen as the smartest guy in the room!

You may have received a 4.0 at Harvard but if that's not what your company needs from you then they don't care.

If you adopt an attitude that says, "I'm better than menial tasks and I can run this company better than anyone" you're just going to alienate everyone. It reminds me of a commercial where a young woman comes into the office of a new hire and says "We've got a problem and we need you!" While walking down the hall the new hire in his expensive suit is looking smug and adjusting his tie. You can see the, I'm-going-to-wow-them attitude on his face. Suddenly they arrive in the shipping department and the woman tells him they are behind and need him to help make labels for the boxes. The young man says, "But you don't understand, I'm an MBA!" And the woman replies, "Oh, you're an MBA? Well then, I'm going to have to show you how to do it."

You may have all the talent and brains to perform at the highest levels in any company and if you display them at the right time with the right attitude it can take you farther than you may have ever imagined. But it doesn't take a genius to perform 99% of the job responsibilities for any position in any company so don't rely only on your intelligence. If you can read this book then you are smart enough to learn what your company needs from you, so go do it. Do it to the very best of your ability and do it with an attitude of helping to improve yourself and the company.

Common sense and a strong work ethic are equal to, possibly greater than, a 4.0 from an ivy-league university. So don't let your lack of education - nor your abundance of education - hold you back.

Hungry:

Speaking of education, when I was in third grade I was given a test that measured the level at which I could perform reading and math. After the test, I was taken out into the hall where I spoke to some of the people who monitored the exam.

I was very worried because I was the only kid in my class who had to go into the hall. In my school it was never a good thing. However, in this case, it wasn't bad. The test people said I did very well on the exam and asked me if I wanted to move to the 5th grade. They told me to take some papers home to my family and have my mom sign it if I wanted to move up.

My mom and I discussed it together and she called my grandparents to share the news with them. There was a long discussion and many questions and comments about what it would be like for me if I moved up. I was shy and very small for my age and was already picked on by lots of kids in my third-grade class, my mom worried about how kids that were two years older would pick on me in their class. She talked to me about it and we discussed how I would get out of school sooner - I loved that idea - but it was also mentioned that I would probably always be smaller than the kids in the class and may have to endure some "teasing" through most of the remaining grades. I hated that idea because I was already being "teased" (which meant bullied/beat up) in the third grade. We wrestled with the idea for a couple of days and finally agreed that in the long run it was better for me to stay with my friends and with the kids my own age.

I'm sharing this story to illustrate what we mean when we say "hungry". In the story I was hungry for three things: I was hungry to be challenged in school, I was

hungry to get through school sooner, and I was hungry to

be accepted. In the end, my hunger to be accepted won.

In your life you have things you hunger for too. Only

you can answer what those things are but they consume

much of your thoughts. It's your hunger for these things

that drive you! Do not let that hunger get away from you

but do curb your cravings. Here's what I mean: do not

be afraid to try something as long as you know you can

get back to where you were with no significant

repercussions.

If I had pushed to go to the fifth grade then I might have

really enjoyed the challenge of tougher school

assignments. If I had not performed as well as expected

or if the social pressures of trying to "fit in" had caused

me to suffer then I could've returned to the 3rd grade. At

this point I'll never know and no one said it was an option. I think if I had really been hungry to move up I would've pushed or asked. I don't know. But you can learn from that mistake.

If you are not making an effort to get what you hunger for it might be because you're fearful of losing what is already on your plate. Please don't let that stop you. Venture to try something with a different flavor and see how it tastes. If you like it and it is good for you then keep eating. If it doesn't sit well in your stomach, then you can go back to what you were originally eating. Don't be afraid to try new things but whenever possible try to secure what you already have.

Here's a true story that illustrates exactly what I'm saying: Back in the 1970's I knew an "uneducated" man who worked for a landscaping company. He understood how the business worked and what his boss needed from him and often performed his responsibilities on his own or while overseeing a few other workers. After many years he found out that the company was going to drop some of the customers in the northern part of the region where they served because it wasn't economical enough to send a crew to that area.

My friend approached his boss (the owner) and told him he would like to try to start his own company to serve those customers who would be dropped. He was quick to point out that he was not trying to "steal" customers and wanted to know if he could have the company's blessing. In fact, he asked if he could have his job back should things not work out for him. You may be surprised to know that his current employer not only gave him his blessing but assured him that he would always have a job if he needed one! (You'll never know if you don't ask!)

The next day he went to all of the customers who were being dropped by the current landscaper and asked if they would give him their business. Each one of them signed an affidavit and he took those to the bank to get a loan to buy the equipment he needed. He had only one setback as he started his new business; he had to borrow a little more money the next month to cover his payroll. After the second month he was in the black and stayed there.

 He grew that company into one of the most renowned landscaping companies in all of South Florida and anyone who was anybody in the elite set used my friend's company to landscape their multi-million dollar homes! And speaking of millions, my friend made millions over the years and retired comfortably after passing the business onto his son!

There are opportunities out there for anyone hungry enough to go after them. You have only to ask yourself this question: Am I hungry enough to try? If the answer to that question is yes, then get out there and start devouring!

Chapter Four's Advice for Life

There is nothing wrong with getting paid for your services.

Poor is not glamorous.

Know your finances.

Spend wisely

Seek to improve your own situation.

Keep setting new goals.

Stay committed.

You are not "better" than anyone else, nor are they "better" than you.

You are not above performing any honest, morally-correct task.

Get along with others.

Stay hungry for what you want.

Have balance in your life.

Believe in yourself.

Chapter 5

<u>Bagging the Elephant</u>

"This is the kid, calls me 59 days in a row; wants to be a player. There ought to be a picture of you in the dictionary under persistence kid." –Gordon Gekko

Every industry has its giant. In most cases, the giant is the largest and most sought after customer but in some cases "the giant" may not actually be the largest in the terms of size or capital; this customer may have the largest amount of influence within your industry. It's the one customer that you know if you can bring them on board will mean big things for you in the future. You know that just by making them part of your clientele you will be recognized, and possibly rewarded, by your own company and other customers will follow the lead of this "giant". In the parlance of the big-game hunters you've just "bagged the elephant".

Rarely does someone bag the elephant the first time they go hunting. Oh sure, there are some lucky few that happen to be standing around when the opportunity presents itself and they hit the target without even taking aim. But the real hunters know that is not going to happen on a regular basis. It takes some practice and experience in the hunt before most folks can even hope to "bag the elephant". The prudent hunter will plan their attack. They'll know where they are going to position themselves, what kind of "weapons" they will hunt with and what will entice their target into their territory.

To properly prepare will take planning and persistence because most elephants, like other big game, are elusive and difficult to "take down".

We hope you will forgive the vernacular we've used so far because we're not really fond of the idea of referring to a company's products and services as "weapons" nor do we like the idea of "taking down" a customer. But it does accurately describe the analogy of "Bagging the Elephant".

The important thing we want to focus on here is the
necessity of persistence. Some folks perceive the idea of
persistence and being "pushy". We think there is a
difference between being pushy and behaving in a
professionally persistent manner. Pushy doesn't put
much thought in how the potential customer may feel
about the interaction nor does it care what may be the
greater concerns of the customer. Pushy is only
concerned about itself. "Professionally persistent" on
the other hand, means being very concerned about the
customer's feelings and needs. It doesn't put itself first
but always looks for ways to be helpful to the customer,
even when the customer doesn't move in the hoped for
direction.

We need to share that the phrase "professionally
persistent" is not ours. We cannot confirm its origin but

in the interest of full disclosure we wanted to share that someone else coined the phrase. But we like it and are going to share with you how we define it and what it has meant when it comes to serving our customers and "Bagging the Elephant".

Earlier we mentioned that bagging the elephant doesn't always mean the largest potential customer. It's probably only fair to also say that in some cases, there may be multiple "elephants". That's the case in our industry. Some of our customers are really very large multi-million-dollar customers but the influence of the individual working in the office may not be as significant as someone working for a much smaller institution. You may be familiar with how to determine the leader in a situation. If not, here's how you can determine who has the most influence in a meeting and whom the group is most likely to follow. During the meeting pay attention to when the conversation gets most quiet and when folks are paying the most attention to one person. When you can identify the individual that most of the attendees are quieting down to listen to then you've identified the leader of that group and the person who has the most influence. In some cases, the leader may be a "de facto leader" with no real title or authority in regard to position, but they wield the most influence, and what they say should happen is the direction most implementations move.

It will be prudent for you to determine within your own industry who are the elephants. What you want to do is identify the customer(s) that all other customers will say, "If they're doing it, then we need to be doing it too." Every industry has at least one. And, we should mention, every industry has at least one customer who will never follow the elephant simply because the elephant is "doing it." If you know who that customer is then bring them on board before your elephant.

Once you've identified your elephant(s) you'll want to get to know them inside and out. Who makes the decisions? What does that person like to do professionally and personally? What is the most important thing to the decision maker in regards to their professional partners? You will use all of this information as you seek to build a relationship focused on serving their needs as a professional partner.

During this process it will be extremely important that you not allow the focus on your elephant to take too much away from other potential customers. In fact, use the other customers to experiment with ways you can more effectively reach out to your elephant. You may discover new ways of performing your job that brings tremendous success! However, in all cases, do not treat your customers as if they are unimportant or simply a sacrificial lamb. No sale is too small not to have importance. During this entire process you are building your reputation within your industry. The image you want to project to the industry is the image you need to project to each customer.

No customer should ever be treated as unimportant in regards to their needs. A sale is a sale and, in some cases, the little sale may be just the right level of success you need to allow you to perfect your message and your service to every customer. We believe it can be easier to serve multiple small customers while building yourself into a power house to marvelously serve your largest or most influential customers. If you make a mistake with the elephant you may not ever get a second chance but if you make a mistake with a smaller customer it can help you identify what never do to again.

While we're on the subject of mistakes, allow us to share not to be afraid of them. Yes, it's always better for you and your customers to get everything perfect the first time. However, there are some cases when a mistake will allow you to show your clients how responsive you are and how well you get a problem resolved. Once a client knows they can count on you to get their issue resolved in a timely and accurate manner, it can result in a level of loyalty that can be very difficult for your competition to break.

Let's get back to being professionally persistent. The best way for us to describe this is to use a personal example using a couple of different clients we served together in our industry.

The first is what happened with a very prestigious potential customer but smaller in volume than other potential customers we were targeting. This prestigious "elephant" was regarded by the industry as an important client but they were not the largest. They were purported as only agreeing to work with whom they perceived as the biggest and the best because they perceived themselves as the biggest and the best. They also had very long-time relationships with their current providers and breaking that loyalty was going to be very difficult.

My co-author and I began the process of learning as much as we could about the current providers the potential customer worked with and what they were receiving from them. With a desire to focus on what our company offered and - not to negatively market against our competition - we created a presentation that clearly identified who we were and what we had to offer. We knew going in that we could not present ourselves as the biggest because we held the position of being third-largest in our industry. However, we suspected our potential client didn't even know we were that big. We also focused on areas where we knew we performed as number one and we brought statistical evidence that pointed to our superiority in those areas. Again, our focus was on what our company offered and where we performed exceptionally well. We did not mention our competitors, nor did we try to draw attention to a comparison between us and the current provider; we allowed the customer to do this on their own, although we were very clear in some areas that what we did was unique to the industry. We prepared all of the documentation that supported our strengths and even compiled a list of current clients we served knowing that this "elephant" would be impressed by some of our current clientele.

On the day of the presentation we arrived early and discussed our game plan before our meeting trying to prepare for any unexpected questions or obstacles. Well, the presentation went swimmingly and the client was thoroughly impressed and even commented on all of the areas we pointed out were areas where we excelled. They admitted they were impressed and told us they didn't know all of these things about our company. We were confident we had won them over and asked for the business. They told us no. We asked where we could improve to earn their business and they couldn't really provide us an answer. In a nutshell, they told us they only work with the biggest and the best and they felt their current provider already held that distinction.

It's important at this point to mention that we don't work in a one-call close industry. If we did we would've pointed out more aggressively some of the obvious comparative differences and pushed for a decision based on the obvious superiority of our company. Some may ask why we didn't do that even in the relationship-based business we work. Well, precisely because its relationship based. It was obvious to us that although we impressed them we hadn't yet broken the impression they had of their current provider. We asked them if they would be willing to continue to meet with us every 3-6 months and they agreed.

So we knew we needed to continue to provide information that showed we brought more value to them than their current provider and continue to emphasize where we were superior to their current provider. Over the next few months we gathered as much information as we could and prepared for our next meeting with our "elephant". In the meantime, we continued to work with other much smaller less "prestigious" customers, although we never considered them less important than any other customer!

During our next visit we shared with our "elephant" more, but different, information regarding industry trends and how we performed in additional areas. We mentioned other customers with whom we had created a professional relationship since our last meeting and shared why they chose to work with our company. It was a good meeting and at the end we asked for the business. They told us no.

I could drag this out but suffice to say that this process continued for over a year. We continued to meet with this potential client once quarterly and continued to provide unique pieces of information regarding our industry and shared details regarding the inner workings of our business philosophy. We provided the occasional article on a subject we knew our contact found interesting and we built the relationship. On one occasion, our contact even commented on how valuable the information we brought to him was and how he looked forward to our meetings because he never considered them a waste of his time because he knew he was going to learn something new. Over time, we successfully convinced our "elephant" that we were the better provider even though we weren't the biggest in the industry. We never pointed out that he wasn't the biggest but we treated him as if he were the biggest; which is how we treat all of our clients. In the end, we bagged our elephant!

But we didn't bag this elephant without serious effort and a commitment to being professionally persistent! There will be times when you will think the effort is never going to pay off. There will be times when you want to just quit, close your bag and just let your elephant get away. You can't do that! Keep your eye on the target and find new ways to approach it. A winning attitude is willing to put in the difficult hours and find creative and unique ways to share their offerings to potential customers until they say "yes". All it takes is persistence. Do you have it in you to be unrelentingly,

but professionally, persistent?

Chapter Five's Advice for Life

Be "professionally persistent"

Always bring value to those with whom you interact

Plan your approach

Look for new approaches to old issues

Learn how to sell

Mistakes can give you an opportunity to show responsiveness and build loyalty

Respond to others as quickly as possible

Get rid of anything that causes stagnation

Eliminate distractions

Do not allow intimidation to stop you from pursuing your goal

The largest is not always the best or the most influential

Learn the needs of others and fill those needs

Chapter 6

<u>Controlling your Emotions</u>

"Don't get emotional." – Gordon Gekko

When a car Salesperson asks you if you would like to "test drive" the car you've been looking at it isn't so you can only learn more about the car. Yes, the salesperson wants you to experience the handling and to learn about the "feel" of the car and how it fits you in relation to your height. Yes, they want you to feel the steering wheel in your hand and reach out to touch the stereo. They even want you to see the color of the instrument panel where you find the speedometer and fuel gauge, and look at how big the trunk and glove compartments are and how much you can store there. They want you to experience all of the whistles and bells of the car because they know that's when you will get emotional about the purchase.

The same is true for a real-estate salesperson. When you look at a house and start talking about how you will place the furniture in a room or what you will put on the walls then you've "taken ownership" of the home in your mind. You've gotten emotional about the house and they know you're one step closer to making an offer.

We all make decisions based on emotion and then justify the decision with logic and reason. Emotion is an important part of purchasing. However, it should not be an important part of selling. And nearly every transaction involves selling someone on something.

When a salesperson gets emotional about a sale it can lead to trouble. The sound of desperation in your voice can lead to someone not trusting you or simply backing out because they know it's too important to you. You would be surprised by the number of people who will decide not to work with you because they like the feeling of keeping something from you that they know is important to you. It's not most people but it applies to some.

Don't get us wrong. We're not saying you should be robotic in the way you approach a deal or a selling opportunity. And certainly you want to express any natural emotion that would make you human in the eyes of your client. What we're saying is not to allow the deal to be the thing that consumes you so completely that you can't concentrate on other tasks or opportunities. We once heard a popular sales guru say that when a customer agreed to sign on the dotted line it was imperative for the salesperson not to show any emotion regarding the transaction. It was strongly suggested that the sales professional monitor their voice so as not to let it appear eager or excited about the success.

Let's make sure we are clear. Again, we're not saying you should never show emotion nor be happy when a sale is made but you do want to temper your emotion. The advice above about controlling your voice at the time a sale is made is excellent in those one-on-one, in-the-home, one-call closes such as alarm systems, cutlery or any other product that meets that description. But if you work in a relationship based business where you may have been courting a potential client for months, or even years, then a little emotion to fit the circumstance may be necessary.

There have been times when we have courted a potential customer for years and showed them various products or services our company offers each time we met. In some cases, we may have shown them a particular product several times over the course of those years to display enhancements we've made to the system and how it will benefit them if they choose to use it. Sometimes, after demonstrating those products and discussing our company, the potential client will have told us they are looking into other providers but to check back with them in a few weeks and they'll be ready to decide.

After those few weeks have passed and we would make the call to the customer and you could hear in their voice the excitement of anticipation expecting to hear our excitement at their announcement they had chosen to use our systems. Now, at those times it is a good idea to show some genuine emotion regarding how happy you are that they made the decision to work with you, but you should always frame it in a way that expresses how happy they will be that they've made the decision. "Oh, that's wonderful! I know you're going to be happy with the improvements this will bring to you!" Is an example. You want to invoke in them the emotion of confidence in you and your company and not just that you secured a win.

A winner knows this is not the only success that will come to them. A winner will make their client feel like the most important in the room and will treat them with the same level of emotion and respect they treat every person but a winner does not tie their self-worth, and the emotion that comes with it, to only one customer.

In the last chapter we discussed the benefits of "bagging the elephant" and how you should remain professionally persistent as you work to bring them into a relationship with you and your company. Please know we understand that it is difficult to work diligently to land a particular customer and spend many hours between meetings preparing and not get emotional about the potential of bringing your "elephant" into the fold. Again, were not saying you should be robotic or uncaring in the way you approach your potential customers. In fact, if you tried to do that you would probably run a greater risk of losing the customer and turning them away from you rather than turning them toward you. You want your customer to view you as a human with feelings. When they can see you as a person they are more likely to allow their emotions to direct their decisions toward a yes because we don't want to hurt people we like. If your potential customer likes you the probability of them working with you is much higher than if they don't like you. Seeing you as human with normal emotions is a step in that direction.

Now that we've said that, you may be asking yourself what we mean when we say "don't get emotional". Forgive the cliché but what we're saying is not to put all of your eggs in one basket. If you've tied so much of your time into only one account as THE ACCOUNT that will make or break your career then you are getting too emotional. Even if you fully understand that not landing the account will not result in your dismissal then you are still setting yourself up for a major let down. A blow like that, after you've invested so much time and energy and believed there was no way the customer could say no, could have disastrous results in your ability to move forward with belief in yourself and your abilities to perform. People who've invested the kind of emotion we're talking about into their potential customers have suffered from depression, ulcers, and other physical and emotional setbacks when the customer they put so much emotional effort into says they are moving in a different direction.

Sometimes you need to be willing to let a potential client go in order to hold on to your own sanity and preserve any possibility of a future relationship. Overly emotional sales professionals have been known to let their negative response to a lost sale keep them from maintaining an attitude of professionalism that preserves the ability to move forward with the potential customer in the future.

Imagine for a minute that you are a life-long fan of an ever-losing sporting franchise and you are given the opportunity to purchase the team at a rock-bottom price. You decide to buy the team and move forward with building the team into the winning franchise you always wanted it to be. After interviewing all of the players and existing coaching staff and watching practices, you have determined that you will have to make changes that will require you to cut your favorite player. You have followed this player for years. You know his statistics, you wear his jersey, and you have read every article about the player ever written. You know his family, his hobbies and what he likes to do in the off-season. And to add to the problem, he happens to be the most popular player on your team. Needless to say, you are distraught over the idea of having to cut this player. By cutting the player you are going to upset other team members and you know you will anger many other fans who have been just as loyal to the franchise as you have been. What do you do?

Now think about the scenario mentioned above and decide what you would do, what you would really do, under those circumstances.

Are you willing to place the player into a position where he will likely have to either take a serious cut in salary from another team or leave the sport completely? Are you prepared to cut the player knowing how the fans and team members are going to react? Are you prepared to allow the player, who once was your idol whom you cared about and supported for years (even to the point of wearing his number), get away from your team and risk never working with him again?

If you can answer "yes" to those questions with confidence, knowing that what you're doing is in the best interest of the future of your franchise, then you have the right emotional response of a winner who is prepared to make the tough decisions to sometimes let a customer go if they are dragging you down and/or keeping you from adequately serving other clients of your company. Your separation from the customer doesn't have to be permanent. But you have other clients on whom to focus your energy and they deserve your attention toward service too!

Keep in mind, a winner learns to control their emotion and knows where to direct it. You don't want to be unemotional but you do want to keep your emotions in check while increasing the emotions of your potential customer toward the benefits of your company's products and services. Get them excited about working with you and only allow your emotional response to be reflected as an excitement for them and the benefits they will yield. When you can focus on the benefits they will gain by working with you and what they will lose if they say "no", then you have the winning attitude that will allow you to keep moving forward when the occasional loss comes your way.

Professionally speaking - no matter the size of the prize, never become emotionally attached to it!

Chapter Six's Advice for Life

Everyone sells something

Control your emotions

Be human, it's okay to express your feelings in a healthy manner

Do what you love (or at least what makes you happy; if it's legal)

Know where to direct your emotions

Never show desperation

Have an escape plan

Follow your intuition

Be resilient

Keep a positive mental attitude

Chapter 7

<u>Perks</u>

"You do well kid and you're going to get lots and lots of perks!" – Gordon Gekko

Most business professionals consider perks to be part of their compensation. In fact, most companies consider perks part of their compensation package. But many folks don't take into consideration the perks they may receive when accepting a position nor do they consider using perks as part of the negotiation process for an acceptable compensation package.

Oh sure, many will ask about the insurance coverage and what kind of "matching" contribution the company will make to the 401K plan but how many discuss other types of perks over and above those things? Often, when the perks that associate a specific position are taken into consideration, one will find that the position is far more lucrative to them for reasons over and above just the salary component. If for example your company contributes to the 401k without you having to also contribute then you can add that percentage to your salary. It's income for you; you just won't see it until you retire.

We're going to take a look at some perks offered by many companies to employees at various stages of position within an organization. For the purpose of this writing we will focus on those perks that are often made available from mid-management down. Some of the perks we will discuss may only be something to consider if you are a sales professional but all are available at various companies depending on what position you will hold and how badly they want to employ you. What we want you to take into consideration and remember as you discuss and negotiate with a company your potential compensation package is this: the best time to negotiate for additional perks or higher salary is either before you're hired or after a huge success.

We're going to start with something that's a bit cliché but for many folks can be a perk that offers a sense of comfort," the key to the executive washroom". Okay, we're willing to admit that many "executive washrooms" no longer need a key but this type of privacy can be afforded to many in a management position. It may not take the form of a key but it could be placement of your office or work space on a specific floor reserved for the higher levels of management. It could also mean that you have your own private bathroom right there in your office. The perk is available at many companies and should not be excluded from your negotiation. It's important enough to so many that even teachers have staff bathrooms and teacher's lounges in the schools.

Your privacy and comfort can be an important thing to you so don't overlook this option.

Similarly, you may want to negotiate where your office will be located. As we mentioned many organizations have a spot designated for those at the higher level. It doesn't mean you have to hold that position. Perhaps they will consider moving someone with more seniority to that level so you can have their "old office". Either way, you want the best you can get right from the start so don't be afraid to ask what they can do for you. The worst they can say is "no".

Here's one that many folks never consider: Paid Time Off (PTO). It's not uncommon for many companies to offer a two-week vacation and six sick days to most of their employees. But consider what additional time off can mean to you and your family. It may not be unreasonable to ask for additional days of vacation as part of your hire. If they won't do it as a result of your position then you may want to consider negotiating specific advancement associated with specific results (this works really well in a sales position). For example, if you exceed your first-year goals by 50% then you will be promoted to the next level and have additional PTO added to your compensation, along with a salary increase. If you meet your goals then you've proven to the company you're worth it! If you don't reach your goals, the company is not out anything they weren't willing to give to you anyway. If you don't want the promotion, then ask for a title and the perks that come with the higher level. Companies are not typically unwilling to reward their most successful employees, just be reasonable in your request. And even if your request is not reasonable, they'll let you know.

Here's something to consider but is difficult to obtain. It works best of you're working for a non-profit or not-for-profit organization that contributes to their employees retirement. Ask if they will contribute a percentage of your base salary (but not from your salary) to the retirement plan on your behalf. For example, ask if they will contribute 3% of your salary to the 401K without you having to contribute at all. If you can get them to agree to that, then it's like getting a 3% raise that's tucked away for you to use in the future. Also, as your salary grows, so does the amount your company is contributing. It's like getting two raises.

If you work as a revenue generator for the company or can show how your efforts specifically benefitted the company's revenue then don't be afraid to negotiate a bonus. Bonuses are almost always paid based on specific achievements by the company as a whole and are sometimes divided among every employee as a "gain share" bonus. If you are specifically involved in the generation of that revenue then your bonus should be tied to your specific efforts. Before you move in this direction be sure you are willing to stand behind your own skills and abilities. However, if you can show that you earned (or saved) the company money then a percentage of that should be in your pocket. In a sales position this perk is almost always built into the position but percentages can be negotiated, so don't be afraid to ask for a bigger percentage. If you're bringing it in for them they are not going to want to see you leave. If you can't get a larger percentage then ask for the key to the executive washroom. I think you see where we're going with this – you need to ask for something that represents your value to the company.

This is probably a good spot to provide a word of caution regarding the negotiation process. Again, the best time to negotiate is before you're hired or after a huge success but that doesn't mean you do it every time you have a huge success, nor does it mean you should be demanding during the negotiation process. We heard of a woman who was very successful for her company and generated millions of dollars in sales. At her last sale which exceeded a million dollars for a single sale, she was promptly dismissed. There was no indication she was unscrupulous in her process for landing the deal nor was the client unhappy with her service. In fact, there was no reasonable justification for her dismissal.

Although this was a blow to the sales woman's ego she was compensated handsomely for the successes she had previously brought to the company and for the last success. In fact, her severance was "life changing" and the amount made her a multi-millionaire. The reason we are pointing this out is to let you know that no company is going to be unreasonable in their negotiations with you but they may be unwavering. You never want to push so hard that you cause damage to your reputation or security with the company.

With that said, let's look at a few other things you will want to consider in regard to the perks of a position or company.

Will the company provide you with business equipment that you can use personally as well for business purposes? One of the immediate items that comes to mind is a laptop computer or cell phone. If you have those things and can use them for personal reasons they can save you money in other areas. For example, if you have a cell phone that is paid for by the company, but they will allow your personal use of it at no charge, then you have a way to communicate with family and friends at no cost to you. If the phone comes with a data plan then the benefit only increases because now you can research and entertain yourself without a single dime coming from your own pocketbook. That's money you can spend somewhere else. With iPads and other devices becoming increasingly popular in the business realm this benefit of using company-provided equipment for personal use only increases the value to you, so negotiate this as part of your compensation.

Another item often made available to certain positions is a company car. The company will offer this because it's cheaper for them to pay for the lease or monthly payment to own rather than compensate you on a per-mile charge. The per-mile charge is almost always a money maker because the amount exceeds what you pay for gas and maintenance, including insurance. However, many companies have moved toward providing a car to their traveling employees because it saves them money. If you have a company car then you'll want to ensure you can use it for personal use too. The obvious savings is that you won't have a car to pay for yourself but you will have one to use. In most cases, the company will also provide a fuel card to use with the vehicle or they will reimburse you the cost of gas. If this is the case then you are simply adding more money to your own account rather than putting it into the use of a vehicle. It's a perk that can mean thousands of dollars of savings to you and your family. At the most, it should only cost you a set amount to be taxed per-mile of personal driving. The savings to you more than covers the amount you will owe in tax. If you are provided a car make sure you're allowed personal use of the vehicle.

Some other travel related perks are per-diems for meals while on the road. In some cases, a company will allocate an amount you can spend for each meal and if you don't spend that much you get to keep the difference. Depending on the amount and how much travel you perform, that can result in hundreds, maybe even thousands, of dollars in your pocket over the course of a year. Consider that you travel three days a week with lunch and dinner covered by the company (breakfast is usually included but since most hotels offer a free breakfast we're not including that cost in this example). If you receive $15 dollars for lunch and $25 for dinner, then you have $40 per day to spend on meals alone. If it's a per-diem that allows you to keep what you don't spend then you'll likely eat mostly fast food at about $10 per meal. When you pocket the remaining $20 per day at three days you're at $60 for the week. If you travel 40 weeks in a year then you're pocketing $2,400 dollars of the company's money. That's a pretty good perk! If you travel and the company provides a per-diem where you can keep what you don't spend, it's a great way to add more money to your own pocket. If they allocate funds but don't allow you to keep the difference (perhaps you have a corporate card they pay for on your behalf), then you still can have some pretty great meals that many others would salivate over if only they could afford them. Meals paid for by the company is a nice perk and not uncommon. If you are traveling, make sure you get them and are happy with the amounts.

One more word on perks for the business traveler; most hotels offer reward points if you stay with their brand and airlines offer points if you fly with them. Do not avoid enrolling in these plans and make sure that your company allows you to keep the points you earn. If the company is paying for your hotel room, and you get to keep the points, that's just more savings to you over the years. You can use those points to stay for free while vacationing or use those points to purchase items you want for yourself or family members. With each point that you use for free vacation stays or merchandise purchased with those points it's like your company buying those items for you or paying for a portion of your vacation. That's a very nice perk and one you should make sure is part of the deal when you travel. It's your time on the road, often away from family and friends, the trinkets and free travel should be part of that sacrifice.

Obviously we could go on about various perks that can be part of any compensation package. There are sports tickets or reserved seating at sporting events or other big-ticket areas. For some positions the use of corporate owned jets and other amenities can be part of the deal. Even recreational activities that can be made part of the job can all play a part in the negotiation process for perks. Regardless of what perks you may get for your position, a winner will always find out what they are and consider them as he or she negotiates their position within the company. You will be surprised at what some companies will provide to their top performers; so never be afraid to ask what they can do for you. Just be sure you can do for them what they need to justify it!

In the end know that your ability to receive perks and negotiate for them is going to be determined by the successes you have and value you bring to your company or the perceived value of a potential employer (this is where a proven track record can help you). The more success you have the more leverage is afforded to you as you negotiate for various perks. And don't be afraid to ask for more than policy will afford. If the company's policy will not allow them to offer you a specific perk, such as increased contributions to a 401K, then ask for something they can make happen. Here's an example involving a friend of ours (We'll call him Bob):

Bob had been very successful at his current employer and had moved up the ladder as well as received a sizable allocation of paid time off and retirement contribution in a 401K and Money Purchase Pension Plan based on the number of years worked.

Over time He was offered a chance to work for a new company in an industry in which he was very familiar serving a territory in which he was very well known and appreciated by his clients. The new company planned to keep him in his established territory which meant he could continue to use his relationship with existing clients to bring them into a business relationship with his new employer.

Bob accepted the position and received a "signing bonus" in stock options. His success was everything he expected it to be and he won the title "Salesperson of the year" his first year with the new company and received an expensive watch in addition to an increase in his salary.

The next year the company was purchased and the stock options Bob was awarded as a signing bonus were cashed in at an increased value and Bob pocketed tens-of-thousands of dollars!

In the meantime, Bob's old company was making some changes and really wanted Bob to return. They approached him to see what it would take to bring him back. Bob agreed to return to his old company but asked for a higher position with a higher salary and, here's the real perk for a top performer, asked not to have his "sabbatical" counted against him; he wanted to return with the same number of years worked as when he left, he did not want to have to start over as if he was at year one of employment. His company agreed.

As a result, Bob returned to his previous employer, received a promotion and a raise and all benefits (including retirement and 401K contributions) continued as if he had never left.

There is no reason why, if you can demonstrate the value you bring to your employer, you can negotiate similar benefits based on your industry. Employers want to keep good employees and will often give them various benefits over and above the standard benefits if they can justify them and if the employee will ask for them. Winners are not afraid to ask and negotiate for what they believe they deserve!

Chapter Seven's Advice for Life

Perks can be as good as money

Never be afraid to ask

Everything is negotiable

Ask for more before you're hired or after a big success

Always ask for more than you expect to receive, but don't be unreasonable

If you exceed expectations, ask for a bonus or a raise

During any negotiation show how you bring value

Never push so hard for more that you damage your relationship or credibility

Chapter 8

<u>Greed is Good!</u>

"Greed, for lack of a better word, is good! – Gordon Gekko

In an earlier chapter we spoke about money and the effort one will often, and many times should, put into obtaining it. We were careful not to make money out to be a god and implied that to make money your sole obsession would be inconsistent with what God would want from you (or anyone) and that you should not sacrifice your relationship with God and loved ones for the sake of money.

It seems odd, with that earlier philosophy in mind, to now suggest that greed is a good thing. Allow us to clarify how we believe that greed can be beneficial to you and to others. We'll do it through an example that shows what a person of significant means can do for others even when they are focused only on themselves. Please keep in mind we are not suggesting you focus only on yourself, but should you be - or become - a shallow, self-obsessed narcissist who cares nothing for others beyond what they can do for you, there is still benefits you can provide to others once you've achieved the pinnacle of success when it comes to wealth.

Before we discuss the example above we would like to talk briefly about an experiment within the United States that attempted to put off the need for greed and the benefits of capitalism. The following story is found in the memoirs of Governor William Bradford:

In 1620 when the Pilgrims first landed at Plymouth they created a commune called "Plymouth Plantation". It was decided that within the commune everyone would work together for the common good of all the inhabitants of the plantation. No one would have their own land nor would anyone provide only for themselves and their immediate family. Instead, all crops would be shared with each person as they had need.

What happened in those first couple of years is a startling commentary on the near non-existent efficacy of socialism. From 1620 through 1623 this "socialist experiment" was a dismal failure. Men feigned sick so they would not be required to work and yet could still benefit from the work of others and the crops they yielded. Unfortunately, there were not many crops that first year and even fewer the second year and by the end of 1622 more than half of the population had died.

In 1623, William Bradford declared the "socialist experiment" shall be abandoned and each man would be given a parcel of land for him and his family to work and provide for themselves. With this new order now in place each man went to work with eagerness, even their wives and children worked the land to produce a large crop that they used to feed themselves and to trade with others who produced a different crop. The yields were tremendous!

The positive results of such a bountiful harvest had to be celebrated, and that celebration was the first Thanksgiving in America! It was their thanks to God for all He had provided to them. Not surprising since the Bible states, "If a man will not work, he shall not eat."

The reason we're pointing this out is to show that a precedent has already been set for the "greed is good" mentality. If it hadn't been for the men who were so greedy they only wanted to work hard and provide for themselves then it's possible, and highly probable, that more of the Pilgrims of Plymouth Plantation would have died as they waited for others to provide for them.

Please note that we are discussing the greed that drove men to work only for themselves. We could have made the statement about the folks who chose to be lazy and sponge off of those who were willing to work hard and share their bounty. However, we believe it is in the best interest of society to want to reap the benefits of your own hard work for yourself and to voluntarily give to others from your blessings.

Having shared the story above we would now like to share with you the benefits that a person of significant wealth can bring to others even though his initial desire was to generate a sizable amount of wealth for himself; to do that we would like to put you into a hypothetical situation where you are the very wealthy person. Let's pretend that you have a job that earns you $10,000,000 annually. We realize that kind of wealth is usually reserved for sports superstars, actors and hedge-fund managers. However, we believe that wealth such as that can be earned by many folks if they just put forth the effort and never give up on their dream. If you think about it you will realize that many authors, managers, and business owners make that kind of money, so it's not implausible you can make that kind of money too!

So, you're a multi-millionaire and you want to make the most of what you have earned. You have multiple houses; one in each time zone near the hot spots for that area. Let's say you have a home in San Diego, one in South Florida, one in New York City, and another in Colorado. You have a custom garage with at least a dozen cars in your "collection" plus you have at least two cars at each home. You have a gorgeous yacht and a large private plane. Wow! This sounds pretty great doesn't it?

Now, some people can handle this kind of wealth and see it as the fruits of their hard work and sacrifice. Others find it harder to accept this kind of wealth and perhaps feel they do not deserve it. The latter emotion usually has the person striving to provide for others via entitlements and they look down on those who don't support that philosophy. Interestingly, those folks often want to provide for others using someone else's money and do not give up much of their own, even though they act as if they despise having it. If you don't believe me, look at the charitable contributions of some of our politicians. Those who usually support a larger government and, arguably, socialism are more often less charitable than those supporting smaller government and private sector production.

Now we're not saying folks of exceedingly high incomes do not give to charity even if they can handle their money with a positive attitude about it. In fact, it's our experience these folks usually give more of their own money away to charity! But we are also saying those folks recognize the benefit their money brings to others even if it's not charity. The following paragraphs will show you how those with significant means benefit others with their money just by spending it on themselves and their own interests.

Going back to our hypothetical that you are a multi-millionaire with all of the toys: expensive houses, collectible cars, a yacht and a plane. Of course you are going to want to take advantage of those things aren't you? You will want to drive your cars and visit your homes, you're going to want to cruise places in your yacht and you will fly to various places in your plane.

So, let us ask you this question: can you be in all the places where your toys are located at one time? Of course not! You can't be at the airport and the marina at the same time, nor can you be at your home in South Florida at the same time you are in your apartment in Manhattan. And since you can't be at all of these places at once you will need to have someone look after them while you're away. This means you will have to hire a property manager to look after your houses to ensure they are safe from burglars or vandals. You will have to pay the marina to dock your yacht and look after it the same way a property manager will look after your houses. You will need to rent a hanger from the airport to store your plane. And you'll need to have a custom garage built to store all of your collectable cars. You will have to use some of your money to pay people to look after your belongings when you're not there. Those are jobs! You're employing people, if not directly, then by hiring a company that provides the service and employees the people. Either way, your wealth is responsible for helping others stay employed just to take care of your stuff.

And it doesn't stop at just looking after them to keep them safe. You're not going to be the person who washes and waxes all of those cars you're going to hire someone to do it for you. The same is true for the boat and the plane. And you'll need someone to keep your houses clean; that's a person or two for each property.

How about the use of these items? It's going to cost you a bundle in fuel just to keep them operated. Will you know how to sail a yacht? Even if you do, are you going to want to be away from the party of people you've invited on board? Probably not, you will probably hire a captain to sail the yacht for you. Are you going to fly the plane? Most likely you will hire a pilot to fly it for you. What about maintenance on those items? The cars will need repairs and preventative maintenance, so will the boat and plane. You're going to need to hire people to take care of that for you too.

Wow! You're spending a lot of money just to have some fun with all of your toys. Are you going to be the person writing those checks? Again, you will most likely hire a personal assistant to handle that for you. So far we've talked about the benefit to others just for enjoying your stuff. How did you earn that money in the first place? In most cases, you probably built a successful business providing a product or service to others. How many people do you employ through your business?

There is no need for us to belabor this point. As you can see there is much benefit offered to many others from wealthy persons who want to enjoy their money. It's simply a fact that a person must spend money to fully take advantage of their wealth and that spending stimulates the economy and benefits others. And that is good for everyone!

So you can now see why we say "greed is good". If it weren't for the greed of one person to earn something for their idea, product, or service, many things may have never been built or provided to the world. If there was nothing gained by the individual for trying to improve on what already exists then why would that person even share their idea, product or service? In many cases they probably wouldn't and we would all suffer as a result. Remember the "Plymouth Plantation" experiment. Few people will actually work only for the common good, and those that will do it initially, will likely lose the motivation when they see nothing extra in it for themselves. History proves this to be true!

Chapter Eight's Advice for Life

Your success will benefit others, even if you didn't intend it.

Do not reward bad behavior or laziness

People who do not work, when they are capable, are a drain on society

The most productive people deserve more of the proceeds

Profitability drives innovation

Competition always brings improvement

Work brings dignity

Ownership brings pride

Voluntarily give to others; benevolence brings blessings

Chapter 9

<u>A Winning Nation</u>

"Now... create, instead of living off the buying and

selling of others." -Carl Fox

In the last chapter we talked about the benefits of having wealth and how it serves to make the lives of others better. It's odd that a movie written about the immoral act of insider trading and corporate greed can serve to be a commentary on the benefits of capitalism. It's possible that many reading this book would argue against capitalism and cite the movie as an example of why. We will give some credence to that argument because people are, inherently, selfish. But it's because of that selfishness that we believe capitalism, even with its imperfections, is a far better economic system than socialism.

Let's look at some of the differences between the two economic programs:

Socialism	Capitalism
Shared Ownership	Private Ownership
Government Run/Controls Production	Market Controlled
Shared Sacrifice	Individual Sacrifice
Assumes Voluntary Cooperation/Productivity	Relies on Voluntary Cooperation/Productivity
Assumes Equal Outcomes for Each Person	Assumes Equal Opportunity for Each Person

This is a very high-level look at the two economic systems. For those readers looking for a more detailed juxtaposition of the two we recommend you put in the effort of additional research. For the purposes of this chapter, what we've listed above, we believe, is enough comparison.

At its core, socialism requires that every person work for the common good of others. We know from the experiment America had with socialism during the Plymouth Plantation years that this simply cannot be relied on for success. People are inherently selfish; socialism pretends this statement isn't true.

The supporters of socialism will say that capitalism creates selfishness through an unnatural competitiveness. But as far as competition is concerned, it always seeks to make things better because the sellers of the goods or services want you to choose them, so they offer more or better options than their competition so that you will have good reason to choose them.

Let's use a couple of examples to illustrate the benefits of competition. The first one will be the United States Postal Service.

Unless you are over 50 you might not remember that at one time the only way to deliver a package from one state to another – without having to deliver it personally – was to send it through the U.S. Postal Service. Back then the customer service was not the same as it is today. Packages were routinely lost or delayed, causing hardship for businesses and heartache for people in general. With every lost business package production was delayed, and with every lost Christmas or birthday package there was a disappointed sender and receiver; we can only imagine how many grandparents and grandchildren cried together over the phone as they realized their loved one's gift would never be received.

Although there are still 19th century laws that protect the USPS when it comes to delivering letters, we now have some competition when it comes to delivering packages (even packages of letters). With UPS and FedEx (plus some other lesser-known options) we now have choice and can hold the deliverer of the package accountable if it does not arrive. This competition has made package delivery more reliable than if we only had one provider of that service.

Let's use one more example that focuses on the issue from a slightly different perspective. Let's use the Student Financial Aid industry. From 1965 until around 1992 if you wanted to borrow a student loan you needed to borrow it from a bank participating in the Federal Family Educational Loan Program. The loans were backed by the federal government up to a percentage of the principle amount because the loans were funded to the students without collateral nor credit history, and the banks were taking a big risk that an 18-year old would pay back their student loans. Without this guarantee, it's probable the banks would not have been willing to participate in the program and take the risk on an unproven borrower.

Around 1992, the government decided it should also be in the student loan business (they were backing the loans after all) and decided to finance student loans with funds from the U.S. Treasury. In order to entice schools to use their loan programs, they offered schools $10 for every loan processed from their school. Naturally, with the promise of a kickback totaling tens of thousands of dollars for some schools, many decided to move to the William D. Ford Federal Direct Loan Program. It should be noted that the "kickback" only lasted one year and then the government decided not to pay the $10 per loan to schools. (Imagine that, the government reneging on a promise and decided to keep more money for itself.) For the next 18 years, the "Direct Loan" (DL) program competed with the "Federal Family Educational Loan Program" (FFELP) for the business of student loans at colleges and universities across the country. During this time, the banks that previously participated had to not only compete with each other for the chance to earn a student's choice as their lender, but now had to compete with the federal government to earn the business at the schools.

This competition led the FFEL Program to make improvements to their processing methods and offer savings to the students as enticement to choose a specific bank as their lender. As a result, the efficacy of processing student loans at colleges choosing the FFEL Program improved, and students were receiving benefits that yielded tremendous savings over the life of their loans in the form of interest rate reductions (as high as 2.50%), principle reductions (as much as 3.33%), or both, along with the payment of certain fees required by the government (Up to 4% more to the student). That's right, some banks would pay, on behalf of the students, the fees mandated by the government if those students chose those banks as their lender! This meant that students received more money up front and had to borrow less to pay for their education because they didn't have to borrow more to cover the fees.

Many schools, motivated by the need for a better processing model and savings for their students, left the

Direct Loan program and returned to the FFEL Program. As a result, the DL program had to create some improvements to their processes, and savings opportunities to students, to keep schools from leaving and returning to the FFEL Program. Competition was making everything better!

Then, in 2010, the Presidential Administration at the time, using laws attached to a healthcare plan, quietly put the lenders out of the federal student loan business. From that time forward, all federal loans would be funded solely by the U.S. Treasury. Unfortunately, without competition for federal student loans, the government removed most of the savings for students; there is a 0.25% interest rate reduction for ACH payments (which is offered because it makes the handling of repayment easier for the government) the fees are back, the big interest-rate reductions are gone, and all principle reductions have been eliminated. As a result, students are paying more for their education now and not just because of tuition increases, but because there is no competition for funding federal loans to create the financial benefits that often come with choice. The government has socialized the federal student loan industry and the people who've suffered the most are the students who need the loans.

From televisions to phones to tax services, the choices we have, and the competition created between the providers of those goods and services has created better, cheaper options for us. All because of competition! I'm sure you can think of other areas where competition has created improvements, can't you?

This, we believe, is one of the biggest drawbacks of socialism. In a socialistic society government controls the production, or at least the proceeds from production, and decides how those proceeds will be spent. For those who support socialism, they believe it will pay for free education, free healthcare, and other free items and services they believe should be made available at no cost to all members of society. This is an admirable goal but it's completely unrealistic. Why? Because people are selfish.

The vast majority of millionaires in the United States are business owners who saw a need and chose to make the sacrifices of time and money to meet that need for others. They saw it as a way to create wealth for themselves and their families because they believed their product or service was something other people would be willing to pay for. Is this a bad thing? No. Because no one in the private sector is forcing those people to buy their product or service. People are exchanging their hard-earned money for it because they see a benefit in having or using it. The exchange is completely voluntary and both parties yield benefit from that exchange.

These same business owners, if faced with having to give the majority of their profits to the government to pay for those "free" things, will likely move their business and production to a country where they do not have to give all of their proceeds away. This kills jobs and hurts the economy in the country they leave. With those businesses gone, the proceeds dwindle and soon there is not enough money to sustain the entitlements of "free" healthcare and education – or any other entitlement. To say this won't happen is naïve. People are selfish and they want as much as they can get for themselves; if they can get it for free, even better. The problem is nothing is ever "free". Someone is paying for it.

Some will say, "We have to keep the selfish people from leaving so we can have the funds to pay for stuff." How do you make that happen? You either give them some special benefit for staying (that's not equitable, is it?) or you force them to stay. If you're going to force them to stay – or at least turn over their business to the government - then you need some way of exerting that force. We could create a military or police presence that metes out punishment for those that try to leave the country or keep what they built. The government could be put in charge of it and the people would be subjected to serve the state under threat of penalty for not complying. Isn't that a vision of a utopian society, being forced to stay in a country and work for the government at a salary they determine is acceptable? That's a lot of power for a select few who run the government. Power corrupts; absolute power, corrupts absolutely. For those who would argue that capitalism is greedy, forcibly taking from others to support a socialist agenda is as greedy as it gets! Despotism anyone?

"That will never happen" some say. Yes, it will. Just look at what socialism/communism has done to the former USSR, Brazil and Venezuela to name a few. The utopian society promised through socialism within these countries (and many others) brought them a tyrannical government where the only beneficiaries of the confiscatory aspects of a socialistic economy were those who ran the government and those who had political ties to that government. The people/subjects did not benefit in the long run.

The sad part is, once a country goes down the path of socialism it's hard to reform the economy. Because when people are dependent on government, regardless of how poor they become, it's hard to break that dependency. This is one reason why so many politicians want to create some form of entitlement, or won't move to remove entitlements, because they know those people receiving them will continue to vote for those politicians providing them. Receiving free stuff does not necessarily mean the giver cares about you or likes you. In some cases, they may simply be trying to obligate you.

Socialism does not foster gratitude it creates an entitlement mindset where more people simply begin to ask, "How much more am I entitled to?" Which leads to more demands for more stuff with an expectation that someone else will provide it to them for "free" because they deserve it. As we said before, people are inherently selfish (some might call it greedy). Capitalism, however, encourages hard work and independence. It creates a desire to be self-sufficient and not rely on others to simply give you something because you believe you're entitled to it. Capitalism requires the greedy person to actually provide a good or service that benefits others, so that those others will pay them to have or use that good or service for improvement to their own lives. The exchange is voluntary and brings benefit to both parties.

In countries where capitalism is the predominant aspect of their economy the lives of all people in those countries is improved. Just look at what we call the "poor" in America. By comparison to those that would be considered poor – or perhaps even middle class – in socialist countries the poor in America are considered "rich". Most of them have televisions, cars, daily food, even cell phones. Items that persons in socialist countries don't have daily if they have them at all. And in many cases, folks in socialist countries are standing in line waiting for the government to provide them their goods.

Please understand, we are not saying that capitalism isn't without its flaws. It is not a perfect economic system either. But capitalism benefits societies in a way that socialism does not because it provides liberty to the people to make their own future, without having to rely on government to dole out everything to them.

The truth is, the most successful countries have an economic system that combines aspects of both socialism and capitalism. And America already has that in place even today. The socialistic aspects of our economy would include, Social Security Payouts, Medicaid, and Medicare, WIC and other aspects of the Welfare System. These are all designed to help people when they need assistance. It is unfortunate that many people abuse this assistance and use it, unnecessarily, to live off these government handouts. But as we mentioned earlier, once a person becomes dependent on government, it's hard to break that dependence; even if it means living in poverty.

We do not want poverty for any person. We want each person to be the very best they can be and to continuously strive to become even better than they are today. Regardless of which country a person lives in we want the very best for them and their families. The intent of this book is to encourage people - and people lead countries, so by extension we also mean countries – to work hard and create opportunity for others. The kind of opportunities that encourage people to work more, not demand more. In the end, those nations that provide freedom to their citizens to produce consumer goods - where the proceeds are regenerated into the economy as well as benefiting those that took the risks to create the goods - are the nations that create the most successful and happiest citizens. They become nations where everyone wants to live. They are winning nations!

Thank you for purchasing this book! We hope that by reading it, you've found some redeeming aspect of wealth, hard work to earn it, and capitalism which provides the opportunity to create it.

Regardless of the caricature of corporate greed found within the personality of Gordon Gekko, this book is about developing a winning attitude. We want you to have an attitude that recognizes:

- Every Dream has a Price
- You have to make necessary sacrifices
- It's good to gain as much information as possible
- You have to stay hungry for success
- You should be persistent and chase the big players
- You need to control your emotions

- Perks are as good as money

- Your success benefits others

- Your success contributes to an economy that improves the nation

Do you recognize these things? Are you willing to follow the advice of this book to change the way you look at your success? Do you understand the things you need to do to succeed? If the answer to those questions is yes, and you follow it up with action, then you have a winning attitude. As a result, you cannot fail – you will learn from things that don't work as originally planned – but that's not failure; and learning, when linked to opportunity and hard work, leads one to succeed.

Now get out there and make it happen.

Here's to your success!

Suggested Reading for Further Growth

Kill the Company – Lisa Bodell

With Winning in Mind – Lanny Bassham

Leadership Lessons of Abraham Lincoln: Strategies, Advice... - Abraham Lincoln

Think and Grow Rich – Napoleon Hill

The Book of Five Rings – Miyamoto Musashi

The Art of War – Sun Tzu

The War of Art – Steven Pressfield

Rich Dad Poor Dad – Robert T Kivosaki

The Accidental Salesperson – Chris Lytle

Beyond Reason: Using Emotion in Negotiating – Roger Fisher & Daniel Shapiro

The Millionaire Next Door – Thomas J Stanley

Steve Jobs – Walter Isaacson

Titan: The Life of John D. Rockefeller, Sr. – Ron Chernow

The House of Morgan: An American Banking... Modern Finance – Ron Chernow

The First Tycoon: The Epic Life of Cornelius Vanderbilt – T.J. Stiles

Who moved my Cheese? – Spencer Johnson M.D.

The Fred Factor – Mark Sanborn

How to Talk to Anyone – Leil Lowndes

High Trust Selling – Todd Duncan

Investigative Selling – Omar Peru

Becoming a Person of Influence – John Maxwell & Jim Dornan

21 Immutable Laws of Leadership – John C. Maxwell

7 Habits of Highly Effective People – Stephen Covey

Sales Essentials – Stephen Schiffman

The Five Love Languages – Gary Chapman

How to Become a Rainmaker – Jeffrey J. Fox

The Holy Bible – 66 Books from various authors; all of them inspired by God!

Biographies

Doug Hess

Doug has spent his whole professional career in higher education. He holds a B.S. and M.S from Indiana State University. He lives with his wife, Misty, and their two boys, Zack and Drew, and their dog, Brownie, in Indiana where he is very involved with the community (he leads several organizations where his boys are involved in sports and other activities) and his local church congregation. He is also the author of the book Words to Ponder.

Dave Bowman

Dave holds a Bachelor of Science in Business Administration. He has worked in various capacities at financial institutions since he was just out of high school, including positions behind the scenes in data processing, as well as in sales where he has been the face of the organization. He was honored to preach part time for 3 years (when his congregation's full-time minister stepped out of the pulpit) and remains actively involved teaching bible classes and consulting with congregations on biblical leadership. He lives in Ohio with his wife, Lynda, their three boys, Joshua, Jacob, and Joseph, along with their dog, Callie. His devotional book, Thoughts on the Cross, *is on track to be published in early 2020.*

44184671R00102

Made in the USA
Middletown, DE
04 May 2019